My Emotions
Emosyon Mwen Yo

HAPPY
KONTAN

A Crabtree Roots Book
Yon Liv Crabtree Rasin

AMY CULLIFORD
JEAN-PIERRE GASTON

Crabtree Publishing
crabtreebooks.com

School-to-Home Support for Caregivers and Teachers

This book helps children grow by letting them practice reading. Here are a few guiding questions to help the reader with building his or her comprehension skills. Possible answers appear here in red.

Before Reading:

- What do I think this book is about?
    - *This book is about feeling happy.*
    - *This book is about what feeling happy looks like.*

- What do I want to learn about this topic?
    - *I want to learn what makes me feel happy.*
    - *I want to learn what feeling happy looks like.*

During Reading:

- I wonder why...
    - *I wonder why we smile when we are happy.*
    - *I wonder why we jump when we are happy.*

- What have I learned so far?
    - *I have learned that playing makes me feel happy.*
    - *I have learned that people laugh when they are happy.*

After Reading:

- What details did I learn about this topic?
    - *I have learned that there are many things that can make people happy.*
    - *I have learned that there are many ways you can look when you feel happy.*

- Read the book again and look for the vocabulary words.
    - *I see the word **hugs** on page 4 and the word **friends** on page 8. The other vocabulary words are found on page 14.*

What makes me **happy**?

Kisa ki fè mwen **kontan**?

Hugs make me happy.

Anbrase fè mwen kontan.

I **smile** when I am happy.

Mwen **souri** lè mwen kontan.

Playing with **friends** makes me happy.

Jwe avèk **zanmi** fè mwen kontan.

I **laugh** when I am happy.

Mwen **ri** lè mwen kontan.

Helping people makes me happy.

Ede moun fè mwen kontan.

I jump when I am happy.

Mwen sote lè mwen kontan.

What makes you happy?

Kisa ki fè ou kontan?

Words to Know
Mo pouw Konnen

friends
zanmi

happy
kontan

hugs
anbrase

laugh
ri

smile
souri

41 Words

What makes me **happy**?

Hugs make me happy.

I **smile** when I am happy.

Playing with **friends** makes me happy.

I **laugh** when I am happy.

Helping people makes me happy.

I jump when I am happy.

What makes you happy?

40 mo

Kisa ki fè mwen **kontan**?

Anbrase fè mwen kontan.

Mwen **souri** lè mwen kontan.

Jwe avèk **zanmi** fè mwen kontan.

Mwen **ri** lè mwen kontan.

Ede moun fè mwen kontan.

Mwen sote lè mwen kontan.

Kisa ki fè ou kontan?

My Emotions

HAPPY

Emosyon Mwen Yo

KONTAN

Written by: Amy Culliford
Designed by: Rhea Wallace
Series Development: James Earley
Proofreader: Ellen Rodger
Educational Consultant: Marie Lemke M.Ed.

Photographs:
Shutterstock: Juan Pablo Gonzaález: cover; Sergey Novikov: p. 1; Ami Parikh: p. 3, 14; pixelheadphoto: p. 5, 14; wavebreakmedia: p. 7, 14; ESBProfessional: p. 8, 14; TinnaPong: p. 9, 14; Africa Studio: p. 11; Monkey Business Images: p. 12; alexei_tm: p. 13

Crabtree Publishing

crabtreebooks.com 800-387-7650

Printed in Canada/042023/CPC20230419

Published in Canada
Crabtree Publishing
616 Welland Ave.
St. Catharines, Ontario
L2M 5V6

Published in the United States
Crabtree Publishing
347 Fifth Avenue,
Suite 1402-145
New York, NY, 10016

Library and Archives Canada Cataloguing in Publication
Available at the Library and Archives Canada

Library of Congress Cataloging-in-Publication Data
Available at the Library of Congress

Paperback: 9781039624580
Ebook: 9781039625426
Epub: 9781039625006